Mit Wörterbuch und Vokabelhilfe

Cordula Tollmien

Englisch lernen mit den Leselöwen Geistergeschichten

Aus dem Deutschen übersetzt von David Ingram
Zeichnungen von Angela Weinhold

W0003426

Loewe

*Der Umwelt zuliebe ist dieses Buch
auf chlorfrei gebleichtem Papier gedruckt.*

ISBN 3-7855-4789-7 – 2. Auflage 2004
© 2003 Loewe Verlag GmbH, Bindlach
Die deutsche Originalausgabe erschien 1994 im Loewe
Verlag unter dem Titel „Leselöwen-Geistergeschichten"
Aus dem Deutschen übersetzt von David Ingram
Umschlagillustration: Angela Weinhold
Reihenlogo: Angelika Stubner
Umschlaggestaltung: Andreas Henze
Gesamtherstellung: sachsendruck GmbH, Plauen
Printed in Germany

www.loewe-verlag.de

Contents

The hungry ghost 11
The ghost of the elephant 22
Aladdin calling Magic Lamp 31
The hospital ghost 39
The Poltergeist 45
The brainwave ghost 57

Liebe Eltern,

unaufhaltsam hält die englische Sprache Einzug in den kindlichen Wortschatz. Was die Sprachwissenschaft nüchtern als Anglizismen betitelt, finden die Kinder überaus spannend. Mit ungebremstem Wissensdurst machen sie sich daran, erste Worte oder Sätze in einer Fremdsprache zu erlernen und zu kommunizieren.

Kinder sind relativ früh mit dem Englischen vertraut, spätestens seit der Einführung des Englischunterrichts an den Grundschulen. Eine Fremdsprache spielerisch, ohne Erfolgszwang, dafür aber mit schnellen Erfolgserlebnissen lernen, so lautet das Motto.
Dieses Prinzip haben wir auch den Englisch-Ausgaben unserer Erstlese-Reihe *Leselöwen* zu Grunde gelegt. In abgeschlossenen Geschichten können die kindlichen Leser ihre ersten Englischkenntnisse anwenden und vertiefen. Die Sprache ist einfach gehalten, die wichtigsten Vokabeln sind im Text markiert und werden in ihrer konkreten Bedeutung am Rand auf Deutsch erklärt. Verben werden dabei gleich in der jeweiligen Person, Adjektive in der flektierten

Form übersetzt. Der Sinn eines Satzes lässt sich so schnell und ohne lästiges Nachschlagen erschließen. Viele Begriffe werden zusätzlich in den Illustrationen durch Wort-Bild-Zuweisungen erläutert.

Im Anhang finden sich sowohl die wichtigsten Vokabeln aus dem Text in alphabetischer Reihenfolge als auch ein speziell dem jeweiligen Thema zu Grunde gelegter Wortschatz auf einer praktischen Ausklappseite.

Die Verben stehen hier im Infinitiv, da an dieser Stelle der Hauptakzent eher auf der Erweiterung des Wortschatzes als auf der Erschließung eines Wortes innerhalb eines Satzes liegt. Dabei werden nicht alle möglichen Bedeutungen im Deutschen angegeben, sondern nur die wichtigsten.

Und wenn Sie mit Ihrem Kind gleichzeitig auch das Hörverständnis und die Sprechfertigkeit trainieren möchten, sind bei Jumbo zu jedem englischen *Leselöwen*-Band die entsprechenden Hörkassetten erhältlich.

Viel Spaß und Erfolg mit
„Englisch lernen mit den Leselöwen"
wünscht Ihnen Ihr

Leselöwen-Englisch-Team

The hungry ghost

It is Tuesday morning.
Sarah and Michael's
mother goes to the fridge. *Kühlschrank*
She opens it. It's empty! *leer*
There isn't anything
apart from one jar of mustard, *abgesehen von; Glas; Senf*
and a five-euro note *Fünf-Euro-Schein*
beside it. *neben*
She is shocked. *schockiert*
All her shopping is gone! *Einkauf; weg*

   "Sarah, Michael! Look at this!"
she shouts.

   "What's the matter, Mummy?" *Was ist los?*
Sarah and Michael ask.

   "Look at this! All the food is *Essen*
gone. Have you got something
to do with this?"

   "No," Sarah and Michael say.

   "And nor have I!" the father *Und ich auch nicht*
says. He is still very sleepy *verschlafen*
because it is so early. *früh*

"All my food is gone!" The mother does not believe what the children say. "Food doesn't just disappear into thin air!"

The mother is a little bit suspicious. She still thinks that Sarah and Michael have something to do with it.

The next day the same thing happens again. All the mother's food is gone! She only finds a five-euro note. This time the mother is even more shocked!

Sarah whispers to Michael: "I have a plan!"

On the way to school, Sarah tells Michael about her idea. When the night comes, she wants to hide in the kitchen with Michael. Then they can find out who takes the food! Michael thinks it is a really good idea.

When their parents are in bed,

Essen; weg

in Luft auflösen

misstrauisch

Fünf-Euro-Schein noch mehr schockiert

flüstert

verstecken

wirklich

the two children creep into the kitchen. They take their bedding with them and cuddle up at the kitchen table. The two children look at the fridge. The room is dark. They are a little bit frightened!

| schleichen |
| Bettzeug |
| kuscheln sich zusammen |
| Kühlschrank; dunkel |
| fürchten sich |

bedding

The only noise they can hear is the buzzing of the fridge. Half an hour later, Sarah and Michael fall asleep.

When they wake up the next morning, the fridge is empty again! And again, there is a five-euro note inside.

The next night, Sarah and Michael decide to watch the fridge a second time. They want to stay awake, but they fall asleep again!

In the middle of the night, a noise wakes them up. They hold their breath and look at the fridge. Nothing. Then the door behind them suddenly closes with a squeaky noise. Sarah and Michael look round. They see something white! It disappears through the door! The two children are very scared!

Geräusch
Summen;
Kühlschrank

schlafen ein

aufwachen

leer

Fünf-Euro-Schein

beschließen

wach bleiben

Mitten in

weckt sie auf
halten ihren
Atem an

plötzlich
quietschenden
Geräusch

verschwindet

erschrocken

Michael shouts out: "Help! A ghost!" Sarah shouts as well.

Their father wakes up and rushes into the kitchen. When the two children tell him about the ghost, he runs outside. But he cannot see anything.

Now the father is angry. "Ghost or not ghost, I want to have my breakfast every day. I want to watch the fridge next time."

Sarah and Michael ask their father if they can watch the fridge with him. "Yes you can," he answers. Their mother decides to watch the fridge as well.

This time everyone is awake. Just before midnight, the door opens quietly. Suddenly a white shape comes into the kitchen and moves along the wall!

Geist; auch

wacht auf

eilt

wütend

Geist

Kühlschrank

beschließt

Mitternacht

leise; Plötzlich

Gestalt
bewegt sich entlang

The father switches on the light. It is Mr Wohlgemuth, their neighbour! He has a white coat on because he sells sausages.

"Well, well!" the father says. He is very surprised. "Why are you here?"

Mr Wohlgemuth feels guilty. "I'm hungry," he says.

schaltet das Licht an	
Nachbar	
Mantel	
Würstchen	
überrascht	
schuldig	

"But you sell sausages. You have lots of sausages!" the mother says.

Michael is angry, too. But he also is a bit sad because it is Mr Wohlgemuth and not a real ghost.

"That's the problem!" Mr Wohlgemuth says. "Everybody likes my sausages so much that all of them are sold!"

Würstchen
wütend
ein bisschen
echter Geist
verkauft

Sarah and Michael nod. Mr Wohlgemuth's sausages taste very good. He is a nice man. Sometimes he gives them sausages for free.

"And now I am very hungry," complains Mr Wohlgemuth.

"I have no time to go shopping. When I start work very early in the morning and clean my

nicken	
Würstchen	
schmecken	
umsonst	
beklagt sich	
früh	
sauber machen	

sausage stand, all the shops are closed. And in the evening when my work is over the shops are closed again. Then I sit at home, and get terribly hungry. In my house I have your key, so that I can keep an eye on your flat when you are away at the weekend. I suppose you want it back now."

   Mr Wohlgemuth takes the key out of his pocket and gives it to Sarah's mother. Then he looks at the floor again. He feels ashamed.

   "I have an idea," the mother says. "Let's all go to bed now. We can give our ghost a few sandwiches now, so he isn't hungry anymore. And tomorrow we can invite Mr Wohlgemuth to have supper with us. Isn't that a good idea?"

sausage stand	Würstchenbude
closed	geschlossen
over	zu Ende
terribly	schrecklich
key; keep an eye on	Schlüssel; im Auge behalten
suppose; want it back	nehme an; wollen ihn zurückhaben
pocket	Tasche
feels ashamed	schämt sich
ghost a few	Geist; ein paar
hungry	hungrig
invite	einladen
supper	Abendbrot

"Oh yes!" Michael and Sarah are very happy. They jump up and hold Mr Wohlgemuth's hand. "Please come to supper! Please!"

"We want to have supper with a real ghost," the father laughs. "So please come."

Mr Wohlgemuth is surprised. Then he laughs as well. "Thank you. I would be very happy to come, and if you want a nice sausage anytime …"

"We'll come to see you," Sarah and Michael say. They are both very glad that Mr Wohlgemuth is a sausage seller, and not a ghost after all!

springen hoch	
Abendbrot	
echten Geist	
überrascht	
auch	
Würstchen	
froh	
Würstchen-verkäufer	
Geist; schließlich	

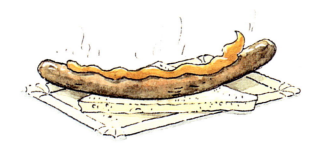

The ghost of the elephant

One day, Mirjam goes to the zoo. She sees an elephant.

He stands all alone in front of his elephant house. He is sad and lonely. The floor is made of concrete, and there are no trees or bushes. Everything is very grey and very sad.

ganz allein

einsam

Beton

Büsche

bushes

Do not feed!

The elephant picks up some hay with his trunk. He waves it in the air, and drops it again. Then he puts his trunk over the railing and touches Mirjam very gently. The elephant looks so sad that Mirjam feels sad, too.

After her visit to the zoo, Mirjam has dreams about the elephant.

One day she walks to school and suddenly she sees a big white elephant in front of her! Mirjam runs over to it. It's the elephant from the zoo! But it is white instead of grey.

The elephant lowers its head, picks up Mirjam gently with its trunk, and puts her on his back.

It is wonderful to sit on the elephant's back! Mirjam feels completely safe.

Heu; Rüssel
schwenkt
lässt fallen
Geländer
berührt; sanft

Besuch

plötzlich

rennt zu ihm hinüber

anstelle von
senkt seinen Kopf
hebt auf

wunderbar

vollkommen sicher

Then the white elephant starts to talk to Mirjam! "I am the ghost of the elephant in the zoo, and of all the other elephants which are locked up. And of circus elephants, too. Do you know how narrow a circus waggon is?"

   Mirjam shakes her head. She has no idea.

ghost	Geist
locked up	eingesperrt
circus elephants	Zirkuselefanten
narrow	eng
circus waggon	Zirkuswagen
shakes her head	schüttelt den Kopf

"It is so narrow that an elephant cannot turn round," the elephant says. "And every day there is a circus show. People clap when we throw a ball or push a pram. We stand on our hind legs and even stand on our heads. People laugh and think that we like to do that."

eng

(Beifall) klatschen
schieben; Kinderwagen
stehen; Hinterbeinen

Mirjam feels ashamed because sometimes she applauds elephants in the circus, too.

The elephant asks her another question: "Our homelands are Africa and Asia. But do you know that there is no more room left for us?"

Mirjam does not know.

"Our homeland now is full of towns, houses, streets and railway lines. And people put us in wildlife parks. Then they drive past us in their cars and stare at us."

For a moment the elephant says nothing. Then he pokes Mirjam gently with his trunk and says to her: "I know those parks. Many elephants die there because they have nothing to eat. Only dry grass, or rubbish out of dustbins. Elephants eat fruit from trees,

schämt sich

klatscht Beifall

kein Platz mehr

Eisenbahnstrecken

Wildparks
fahren an
uns vorbei

starren

knufft

sanft; Rüssel

sterben

trockenes

Abfall; Mülleimern

Früchte

but people cut down all the trees. *fällen*
Elephants drink water. But people poison the water. They *vergiften*
shoot elephants, too. And they *erschießen*
lay traps for them. And when we *stellen ihnen Fallen*
are dead, people break off *tot; brechen ab*
our tusks. And then they *Stoßzähne*
carve little elephants out *schnitzen*
of them."

Mirjam shivers. She feels cold. *zittert*

The white elephant blows *bläst*
warm air at her, so she feels warm again.

"We are kind to people," the *freundlich*
white elephant says. "But people are unkind to us. They think *unfreundlich*
they can live without us. But a *ohne*
life without animals is a very lonely life." *einsames*

The white elephant waves *schwenkt*
his big head left and right, and Mirjam nods. She *nickt*
believes him. She wants

the animals to stay. And especially the elephants.

"Yes," the white elephant says. "You children love us and you understand us. That is why I only appear to you. You are the only person allowed to ride me and to listen to my sad story. The story about elephants dying out and about a world without animals."

bleiben	
besonders	
erscheine	
die reiten darf	
die aussterben	
Welt	

Then the elephant kneels down. He puts Mirjam back on the ground very carefully, with his big trunk. He says: "I must tell you a secret. Children who see white elephants never have bad dreams. They always sleep very well and feel very comfortable. That is a very special present. A present from the elephants to the children."

| kniet nieder |
| zurück |
| Boden; vorsichtig |
| Rüssel |
| Geheimnis |
| angenehm |
| besonderes Geschenk |

trunk

Aladdin calling Magic Lamp

Erwin is a lorry driver. He likes driving and he usually delivers food.

He drives for a big chocolate factory and today his lorry is full of chocolate. The journey takes seven hours, and Erwin is a bit tired. To stay awake, he decides to switch on his radio set. But he doesn't want to talk with the other lorry drivers. He just listens to them. Sometimes it can be very funny.

One of his friends tells a joke. Erwin laughs. Then he suddenly hears a strange voice on the radio set: "Aladdin calling Magic Lamp."

Erwin thinks it is a dream. Then he hears the voice again:

Lastwagenfahrer	
liefert Lebensmittel	
Fabrik	
Reise dauert	
ein bisschen müde; wach zu bleiben; beschließt anzustellen; Funkgerät	
lustig	
plötzlich	
seltsame Stimme	
Zauberlampe	

"Aladdin calling Magic Lamp."
"What's that?" Erwin wonders.
Then again, for a third time:
"Aladdin calling Magic Lamp."
Erwin does not know the voice. It is a strange, sing-song voice, and it is very mysterious. Erwin decides to wait and listen for it to come back again.

wundert sich
Stimme seltsame Singsang-Stimme
geheimnisvoll beschließt; auf sie zu horchen

Yes! There it is again!

"Aladdin calling Magic Lamp," the radio set says. *Funkgerät*

Then Erwin takes the microphone and says: "Magic Lamp here."

"At last!" the strange voice says. *Endlich*

Then it tells Erwin what to do. He has to leave the motorway *Autobahn* and turn left. Then he has *links abbiegen* to go down a road with lots *hinabfahren; Straße* of bends and turn right over *Kurven* a bridge. Then the voice tells *Brücke; Stimme* him to stop at the side of *seitlich von* the road.

Erwin's lorry is right in front of a big brick building. *Backsteingebäude*

The voice says: "Aladdin calling Magic Lamp. Thank you. Over." Then everything is quiet. *Ende; ruhig* Erwin is tired. He puts his head *Kopf* on the steering-wheel and *Lenkrad* soon falls asleep. *schläft bald ein*

The next morning, Erwin wakes up. He is shocked. Where is he? Then he sees an old lady. She tells him how to get back to the motorway. Erwin must deliver his chocolate quickly.

He drives fast, and soon arrives at the supermarket. He goes to the back of the lorry and opens the big door. Then he gets a very big shock: the lorry is empty! Completely empty! All the chocolate is gone! Nothing is left! Not even a single bar of it! Erwin cannot believe his eyes!

wakes up; shocked	wacht auf; schockiert
lady	Frau
get back	zurückkommen
motorway	Autobahn
deliver	ausliefern
lorry	Lastwagen
shock	Schock
empty; Completely	leer; Vollkommen
gone	weg
left; Not even	übrig; Nicht einmal
single bar	einzige Tafel

In a small town with a big brick building two boys called Andreas and Torsten give presents to their school-friends: hundreds of bars of chocolate! Of course, this makes the teachers suspicious. Andreas and Torsten have to go to the headmaster. He asks them where the chocolate is from.

Andreas and Torsten tell the headmaster a very strange story:

The two boys are in the playground when suddenly they find a magic lamp. They rub it and see a genie. They ask the genie for some chocolate. The next day they discover all the chocolate bars in a corner of the playground!

The headmaster does not

Backsteingebäude

Natürlich

misstrauisch

Direktor

seltsame

Schulhof; plötzlich

Zauberlampe
reiben; Flaschengeist

entdecken

Ecke

believe a word of this story, of course. But no one can prove if the story is true or not.
So the headmaster decides to believe Andreas and Torsten.

natürlich; beweisen

Direktor beschließt

It is the same with Erwin. No one can prove that his story is not true. But no one believes him, of course.

the same with	dasselbe mit
prove	beweisen
of course	natürlich

His friends laugh at him. His boss thinks Erwin must work less. Perhaps he is too tired. But Erwin is a good driver, so the boss decides to forget about the chocolate. Erwin's friends soon forget about it as well.

work less. Perhaps	weniger arbeiten; Vielleicht
tired	müde
decides	beschließt
forget about	vergessen
soon	bald
as well	auch

Soon Erwin is the only person who still remembers the strange sing-song voice from his radio set. That mysterious voice!

remembers	erinnert sich
strange sing-song voice	seltsame Singsang-Stimme
radio set	Funkgerät
mysterious	geheimnisvolle

The hospital ghost

Marco is in hospital. In the daytime he is not frightened. Sometimes he is very happy. His brothers and sisters come to visit him and pretend that his wheelchair is a racing car! Sometimes Annika's mother comes and reads him a story. And one day Timo and Carmen paint a picture for him. The nurse thinks it is so good that she hangs it up in the corridor.

   At night, everything is different. The children are all alone. The parents are not there, and the night nurse only comes if there is an emergency. Because the children have to sleep. But lots of children cannot sleep.

*Krankenhaus
bei Tage;
fürchtet sich*

*besuchen;
tun so, als ob*

Rollstuhl

Rennwagen

malen

aufhängt

Flur

anders

ganz allein

Notfall

They lie awake because they are frightened. The room is dark.

Marco lies in bed and stares into the darkness. In the next room, Annika is awake, too. Timo's eyes are closed, but he is not asleep. Bastian is also awake, and Benjamin and Carmen are sad. But they cry quietly so no one can hear them.

liegen wach

fürchten sich

dunkel

starrt

Dunkelheit

geschlossen

eingeschlafen

weinen leise

Then the door opens without a sound and an old woman floats into the room. "Don't be frightened," she says. "I'm the good ghost of this hospital. I'm your hospital angel."

She doesn't look like an angel. She has lots of grey hair and is so fat that it is amazing she can fly at all. But she floats along like a cloud.

lautlos	
schwebt	
fürchtet euch	
Geist	
Krankenhaus; Engel	
sieht aus wie	
Haare	
dick; bewundernswert	
überhaupt	
schwebt; Wolke	

Her eyes are the nicest thing about her. Her eyebrows are not white, but almost black. Her eyes are even darker. When children look into them, they feel like they are floating, too. The hospital angel floats to Marco, Annika, Timo, Carmen, Bastian and Benjamin. She sits down on the edge of the beds very gently, so that she doesn't hurt the children.

She looks at the children, holds their hands and strokes their faces. Big round tears come out of her eyes. The tears are very clear, and when they trickle down her cheeks, the whole room gets very bright and warm. It's like the sun coming out.

Then the sick children feel wonderfully warm and happy.

nicest	schönste
eyebrows	Augenbrauen
darker	dunkler
floating	schweben
hospital	Krankenhaus
edge	Rand
gently	sanft
hurt	verletzt
holds their hands; strokes	hält ihre Hände; streicht
faces; round tears	Gesichter; runde Tränen
clear	klar
trickle; cheeks	tröpfeln; Wangen
whole	ganze
warm	warm
sun coming out	Sonne, die herauskommt
sick	kranken
wonderfully	wundervoll

She cries with them each evening. And then even the sickest children go off into a deep and happy sleep.

weint; jeden

kränksten

tiefen; Schlaf

The Poltergeist

Jakob gets into bed. Then he hears a loud noise above his head, and a strange, dragging sound. He stares at the ceiling. The dragging sound gets louder. Then it stops, but starts again a bit later. Jakob feels his spine tingling. Someone must be in the attic above him. A burglar, perhaps?

   What can he do? His parents are not at home, only his grandfather. But his grandfather watches television every evening. Then Jakob hears a terrible loud bump. He gets a fright. It can't be a burglar. A burglar isn't that loud.

   He must tell his grandfather! But Jakob's grandfather says: "I can't hear anything."

geht ins Bett
Geräusch
seltsames
Scharren; starrt
Zimmerdecke
lauter
ein bisschen später
Rücken prickeln
Dachboden
Einbrecher; vielleicht

schrecklich
Stoß; bekommt einen Schreck

"Come up to my room," Jakob says. The grandfather comes with him. Silence. But then, suddenly, there is a loud, scratching sound! Jakob's grandfather is frightened, too.

"Do you have a torch?" he asks Jakob. "We must take a look."

Jakob has a good torch. It works really well.

The two of them open the attic door. It squeaks very loudly. They are frightened, but they walk bravely into the attic.

Then the grandfather shines the torch around. They can't see anything or hear anything. Then they walk further into the room. The grandfather shines the torch into every corner. Nothing!

komm hoch

Stille

plötzlich

Kratzen

fürchtet sich

Taschenlampe

nachsehen

wirklich gut

Dachbodentür; knarrt

mutig

leuchtet

weiter

in (hinein); Ecke

torch

"Looks like we chased him away," the grandfather whispers.

"Who?" Jakob asks.

"I don't know," the grandfather answers.

He shines the torch up at the roof. They see a loose tile. Just one.

"Hmmm," the grandfather says. "A person can't fit through that hole. Perhaps it was only the wind."

Jakob doesn't believe him. The grandfather gets up on a chair and puts back the tile again.

"There we are," he says. "I think we'll have peace and quiet again now."

But the grandfather is wrong. Jakob goes to bed and falls asleep, too. But in the middle of the night, the scratching starts again!

haben verjagt
flüstert

leuchtet; Taschenlampe
lockeren Dachziegel

hindurchpassen
Loch; Vielleicht

stellt sich

Frieden und Ruhe

mitten in
Kratzen

Jakob sits up in bed with a fright. This time his grandfather hears it as well. He comes into Jakob's room and they listen together.

It's just the same as before: a loud noise, then a scratching sound, and then silence. Then it starts all over again.

Jakob's grandfather thinks it is really strange. But he doesn't want to go back up to the attic.

setzt sich auf; erschrocken	
auch	
genau dasselbe wie zuvor	
Geräusch	
Kratzgeräusch	
Ruhe	
wieder von vorn	
wirklich seltsam	
zurückkehren auf; Dachboden	

Jakob doesn't want
to go up again either.
Half an hour later,
everything is quiet again.   *ruhig*

"We'll check tomorrow,"
the grandfather says.
"Let's sleep first."   *schlafen*

After school, two of Jakob's friends are with him: Jesko and Franziska.

He tells them about the strange noises. Jesko thinks it is a ghost. He says that is why it was so quiet in the attic when Jakob and his grandfather looked there. A ghost knows when people look for it. Franziska also thinks there is a ghost in Jakob's attic.

All four of them – grandfather, Jakob, Jesko and Franziska – search the attic again. But they can't find anything.

"Perhaps you're right about the ghost. I don't believe in them. But all that noise, and then nothing." The grandfather looks around the attic. "I don't know. Perhaps it was just a dream. What do you think, Jakob?"

Jakob shakes his head. He is certain it was not a dream.

seltsamen Geräusche

Geist

ruhig; Dachboden

Geist

Alle vier

suchen ab

Vielleicht hast du Recht

schüttelt den Kopf

sicher

That night, Jesko and Franziska sleep in Jakob's room. They want to know **what the ghost sounds like**. *wie sich der Geist anhört* **Perhaps** *Vielleicht* they can find it. The grandfather thinks it is a good idea. They all sit on Jakob's bed and wait. Everything is very **quiet at first**. *ruhig zunächst*

Suddenly *Plötzlich* Jesko says: "Ssh! I can hear something!" They listen. "It sounds like someone is on the **drainpipe** *Abflussrohr* outside!"

It really sounds like that.

The three of them **creep over** *schleichen hinüber* to the window. They can't see anything.

"We must go outside," Franziska **whispers**. *flüstert*

Jakob whispers: "I'll get my grandfather." His grandfather comes with them.

Franziska isn't frightened. She wants to see what the ghost looks like. And Jakob and Jesko just follow her outside. Jakob takes his torch with him.

isn't frightened	fürchtet sich nicht
ghost	Geist
looks like	aussieht
follow	folgen
torch	Taschenlampe

Outside the house, they can't see anything. Not on the drainpipe either. But then Jakob shines his torch up onto the roof. And then they see it: a little raccoon! When the torch shines on him he stands perfectly still.

"Oh my goodness," the grandfather says. "It's a raccoon. And he's decided to turn our roof into his home. That's not too good."

"Why not?" asks Jakob.

"Because raccoons make so much noise every night that it is impossible to sleep," the grandfather answers. "Our little friend up there is a real nuisance. We must persuade him to move his nest to the forest."

Abflussrohr

Taschenlampe

Waschbär

leuchtet
steht vollkommen ruhig
Ach du meine Güte

entschlossen

nicht so gut

machen so viel Lärm

unmöglich

echter Quälgeist

überzeugen

umziehen

Wald

That is quite easy. The grandfather puts a bit of barbed wire round the drainpipe, so that the raccoon cannot climb up to the roof anymore. Jakob is a bit sad about that. But he is happy that he can sleep in peace again.

And the next summer they find a nest in the forest, in an old tree, with three baby raccoons inside it!

ziemlich

Stacheldraht; Abflussrohr

Waschbär

ein bisschen

in Frieden

The brainwave ghost

Hello, I'm Alwin. You can't see me. You can't usually hear me either. But you can find me everywhere. I like schools. My speciality is brainwaves. And these work best at school.

Spezialität; Geistesblitze funktionieren am besten

Sometimes the teacher asks Julian a question. Julian is my favourite pupil. He's very friendly, but a bit slow. And he's very bad at mathematics.

Lieblingsschüler; freundlich

ein bisschen schlecht in Mathematik

Today the teacher is in a bad mood. Everybody in the class can tell. He asks Julian:

schlecht gelaunt

"Julian, how much is 3 times 37?"

Julian doesn't know, of course. It's quite a difficult question, in fact.

natürlich

ziemlich

tatsächlich

"3 times 37," the teacher repeats. "Well?"

wiederholt

Julian says nothing.

Now I know it's my turn. The teacher mustn't tell Julian off, or try to frighten him.

The teacher says: "If you carry on like this, you will have to stay on after school in detention."

This is where I come in. When people are worried, they can't think straight. Julian needs me urgently. So I send him a brainwave.

bin ich dran	
ausschimpfen	
versuchen; Angst machen	
weitermachst	
noch bleiben	
nachsitzen	
Das ist mein Stichwort.	
besorgt	
klar denke	
braucht; dringend	
Geistesblitz	

"111," Julian says.

The children are really happy. The poor teacher looks upset. | wirklich
ärgerlich

"37 times 27?" he asks. It's an even more difficult question. | sogar noch schwierigere

Julian answers immediately: "999." | sofort

You can't fool Alwin. It's so easy for me. One brainwave, and everything's okay. The children are happy and so am I. And that's what I like best. | hereinlegen
Geistesblitz

das mag ich am meisten

Dein Wörterbuch A–F

A a bit — ein bisschen, ein wenig
a few — ein paar
after all — schließlich
all alone — ganz allein
to be allowed — dürfen
angry — wütend, ärgerlich
anytime — irgendwann
apart from — abgesehen von
asleep — eingeschlafen
at first — zuerst, zunächst

B back — zurück
to believe — glauben
beside — neben

C carefully — vorsichtig
certain — sicher, gewiss
clear — klar, hell, rein, deutlich
comfortable — angenehm, bequem, gemütlich
coming out — herauskommen
completely — vollkommen, völlig
to cry — weinen, schreien, heulen

D	deep	tief
	to decide	beschließen, (sich) entscheiden
	different	anders
	to disappear	verschwinden
	to discover	entdecken
E	each	jede, -r, -s
	early	früh
	empty	leer
	especially	besonders
F	to fall asleep	einschlafen
	favourite	liebste, -r, -s
	fit	passen
	friendly	freundlich
	to follow	folgen
	food	Essen
	to fool	hereinlegen
	to forget about	vergessen
	funny	komisch, lustig
	further	weiter

Dein Wörterbuch G–Q

G	to get back to	zurückkommen zu, zurückkehren zu
	glad	froh
	to go down	hinabfahren, hinab-, hinuntergehen
	gone	weg, vergangen, vorbei
H	head	Kopf
	to hear	hören
I	immediately	sofort
	impossible	unmöglich
	in fact	tatsächlich
	in the middle of	mitten in
	instead of	stattdessen, anstelle von
	into	in (hinein)
	to invite	einladen
	it takes	man braucht
L	less	weniger
	to lie awake	wach liegen
	lonely	einsam

	to look like	aussehen wie
M	to move	bewegen, transportieren, umziehen
N	to need	brauchen
	to nod	nicken
	not even	nicht einmal
O	over	vorbei, zu Ende, Ende
P	to paint	malen
	perhaps	vielleicht
	to persuade	überreden, überzeugen
	to pick up	aufheben
	to pretend	vorgeben, so tun, als ob
	to push	schieben, stoßen, drücken, drängen
Q	quickly	schnell
	quiet	ruhig
	quietly	leise

Dein Wörterbuch Q–Y

Q quite — ganz, ziemlich, völlig

R real — echt, wirklich
really — wirklich
to remember — sich erinnern
to repeat — wiederholen
to ride — reiten

S to search — (ab)suchen
secret — Geheimnis
sick — krank
to sleep — schlafen
soon — bald
special — besondere, -r, -s, außergewöhnlich, -er, -es

to stand — stehen
to stay — bleiben
to stay awake — wach bleiben
strange — seltsam, merkwürdig, fremd
suddenly — plötzlich
sun — Sonne